airline

IDENTITY, DESIGN AND CULTURE

Written and designed by Keith Lovegrove

teNeues

Published in U.S. and Canada by
teNeues Publishing Company
16 West 22nd Street, New York, NY
10010
Telephone 212 627 9090
Fax 212 627 9511
www.teneues.com

Published in Germany by
teNeues Verlag GmbH + Co KG
Am Selder 37, 47906 Kempen,
Germany
Telephone +49 (0) 21 52/916-0
Fax +49 (0) 21 52/916-111
www.teneues.de

Published by arrangement with
Laurence King Publishing
an imprint of Calmann & King Ltd
71 Great Russell Street
London
WC1B 3BP

ISBN 3-8238-5460-7

Printed in Hong Kong

FRONTISPIECE **After routine
maintenance and a thorough
clean, 390 tonnes of All Nippon
Airways Boeing 747 is ready
for action at Kansai
International Airport, Osaka,
Japan, 1998.**

Kimbag

Worldwide air travel is, at its most surreal, a parallel universe. While the airline industry is in contact with terra firma for a certain percentage of its kinetic life, it is also spinning an invisible (and sometimes visible) web of vapour trails around planet Earth. In the last year of the last millennium, approximately 1,500 million airline passengers flew a total of 240 billion kilometres worldwide. In other words, a return trip to the Moon for the population of Denmark. And while engineers and pilots (and statisticians) defy gravity, inside the aluminium fuselage the human culture must be maintained. Fashion, product and interior design, and food are adapted for life at 35,000 feet. In the mid-1930s there were no tiered classes on commercial aircraft – only the rich flew, so there was no reason for segregation or choice. Over the following six decades, as aircraft got bigger, faster and more reliable, more and more people wanted and were able to travel by air. New airlines came (and sometimes went), often opening up original destinations to different types of passenger, but often competing directly with established carriers. With the help of marketing analysts and designers, the commercial aviation industry advanced at high speed. The identity, design and culture of air travel has, in short, adapted, developed and sometimes mutated. This book illustrates and analyses the successful – and occasionally not so successful – results of the airlines' relentless quest to vie for attention.

fashion

A fashion pageant parades from the airport concourse through the air bridge and on to the aircraft; for passengers and crew alike, glamour and flying have always been synonymous. Hollywood scriptwriters and blockbuster bestselling authors continually use the skies as an arena for staging glamorous histrionics. The airline industry is a catwalk for the image makers and the image takers.

Air travel has always been 'fashionable', but until the invention of stewardesses, passengers held the monopoly of the flying fashion-conscious. In 1919, Deutsche Luft-Reederei (the forerunner of Lufthansa) began a regular air service between Berlin and Weimar with the first all-metal winged aircraft, the Junkers F13. The first to cash in on its courageous new venture was the publicity-seeking show-business set. Hans Albert, a blond, swashbuckling film star of the time, posed for photographers in a passenger seat in his dress clothes. Today, the airport arrival/departure publicity shot still has front-page value, although snatched photographs of celebrities in the departure lounge do not have as much glamour as the boarding-steps 'wave and smile' of the 1950s and 60s. Airline publicity and fan-club walls in the 1950s were peppered with stills of Gina Lollabrigida, Raquel Welch and The Beatles disembarking from planes.

Before the Second World War, air stewardesses were a relative luxury. Stewards, however, were an integral part of the service on the 'flying-boats'. In the 'flying dining cars', as they were also

FACING According to a spokesman at Southwest Airlines of Texas in 1973, when stewardesses were interviewed for jobs, he started with their legs and worked up to their faces.

ABOVE American Airlines stewardesses face the press in the mid-1970s.

9

Confab pretence –
a United Airlines stewardess
chats to a passenger in a
simulated cabin of a Douglas
DC-10, 1968.

"We recommend passengers to place cotton wool in their ears to reduce the effects of engine and airscrew noises."

FACING The New York Midnight Follies alight from a Handley Page HP42 on arrival at Croydon Airport, near London, c.1930.

ABOVE Lufthansa flight and ground crew, 1933.

LEFT Fur-clad ladies return to London from a continental skiing trip and disembark from an Imperial Airways Argosy, 1927.

FAR LEFT Standard issue, 1930s.

ABOVE **British European Airways 'lightweight' summer uniform, 1940.**

ABOVE RIGHT **The airline industry's first stewardesses ready for inspection for Boeing Air Transport, 1930.**

FACING **A proud Imperial Airways ground steward stands to attention next to a Handley Page HP42, c.1930.**

OVERLEAF **Ready for action – flight stewards about to go on duty on the Eastern Airlines Silver Sleeper Service from New York to San Francisco; and a stewardess beckons late travellers on board a Trans-Continental flight from Los Angeles, 1930s.**

known, a single steward of 'respectable age' wore a crisp white waiter's jacket and served passengers inflight snacks and drinks. Airships and flying boats gave rise to the nautical descriptions of the airline staff – captain, first officer and steward – and even ground staff wore sailor-collars and caps. Stewardesses today can thank one woman for their career: in 1930, Ellen Church, a registered nurse, convinced Boeing managers that women could work as stewards, so nurses serving aboard the 18-passenger, fabric-covered Boeing 80A became the first female flight attendants in the history of aviation. They wore just-below-the-knee-length A-line skirts, double-breasted jackets, soft cloth hats and very sensible shoes. Swissair was the first European airline to introduce stewardesses in the early 1930s. Lufthansa soon followed and employed stewardesses on board the 40-seater Junkers 90. They wore dark, mid-calf-length A-line skirts, dark ties bearing the company motif – a flying crane – and white box-cut jackets, all topped off with jaunty, fez-style hats bearing the company logo. Lufthansa grasped the concept of corporate identity from the outset and realized that the stewardess could be a symbol for the airline – a walking, talking advertisement.

As with the initial development of the computer industry, commercial air travel grew because of military technology: the north African desert landing strip became Morocco's International Airport; the Avro Lancaster bomber became the Lancastrian and transported the summer-sojourning elite between London and Buenos Aires; and the leather-and-sheepskin-clad USAF

fighter pilot became the TWA captain. Military uniforms were adapted for the new world at peace, though the couturiers' adjustments were minor. The clothes were produced by menswear professionals and cut from masculine twills in regulation blue, grey or green. Over the next decade the uniforms were redesigned, reinvented and restructured. The airlines were continually trying to devise versatile outfits, ones that would be practical yet smart.

The introduction of long-haul multi-seater jets, such as the Boeing 707 in the late 1950s, created new challenges for airlines. Now, with a payload of up to one hundred passengers, new ways had to be found to cope with and entertain large numbers of people during the flight. Safety regulations were introduced which specified the number of flight attendants required for a given type of aircraft according to the number of seats. The calculation was based on the number of passengers an individual cabin staff member could supervise in case of emergency – about 30 passengers per flight attendant. This new passenger handling system had one important consequence: in the past, when it had normally been the captain or first officer who greeted the boarding passengers, it was now the stewardess. She became the public face of the airline, the embodiment of the corporation. How she (or occasionally, he) looked began to become increasingly important – the stewardess was no less than a corporate ambassador. When, in the late 1950s, BOAC introduced Indian stewardesses dressed in saris on their flights to the subcontinent, the corporation assured passengers that Norman Hartnell, designer-in-ordinary to HM The

FACING In 1951, newly appointed BEA stewardesses attended Elizabeth Arden's grooming rooms for demonstrations of beauty tips.

ABOVE Revlon and Clinique abound in the British Airways cabin crew training department, 1970s.

ABOVE RIGHT In 1949, on board a Pan American Boeing Clipper, women could retire to the powder room on the upper deck before luncheon and dinner.

RIGHT Couturier Christian Dior and his catwalk models en route from Paris to Edinburgh, Scotland, to show his collection, on board an Air France aircraft, 1955.

OVERLEAF Two superstructures arrive at Frankfurt Airport, Germany, to adulation; a Convair aircraft and Hollywood actress Jane Mansfield, 1957.

Queen, had been consulted on the choice of colours. Other airlines varied their uniforms, both for practicality and for fashion reasons, but kept propriety securely in mind.

Then, in 1965, an advertising executive named Mary Wells changed the rules of airline fashion by hiring designer Emilio Pucci (himself a decorated Second World War bomber pilot) to design new uniforms for Braniff International's 'hosties'. Sex was the message. Mary Wells put it bluntly: 'When a tired businessman gets on an airplane, we think he ought to be allowed to look at a pretty girl.' Emilio Pucci's clothes were status symbols and adorned some of the most famous and fashionable women of the time. A recipient of the coveted Neiman-Marcus Fashion Award in both 1954 and 1967, his collections were considered avant-garde in style. The Braniff recruitment brochure described the perfect Braniff stewardess: 'A Braniff International hostess is a beautiful person ... a friend to everyone who boards her plane ... She is a model in how to walk, talk, sit, stand, apply make-up properly and style her hair.' In the Pucci uniform the Braniff stewardess turned heads from Dallas to New York and from London to Hong Kong. In 1968, Pucci re-created the Braniff look again by introducing the 'elegant' look, saying: 'The hostesses have two dresses – one in pink and one in plum – to be worn alternatively as they choose. The new Braniff hostess scarf, which can be worn around the neck or over the head, utilizes six shades of red – from palest pink to deep maroon. Shoes and panty hose match the dress color and there is a coat that reverses from pink to plum. The dresses have long sleeves (or short

sleeves in warmer climates), are hemmed above the knees and have a free flowing panel over-skirt in front and back. The fabric is *Trevira*, a new wash and wear wool and polyester blend. For serving time, the girls wear a tunic apron of soft, silvery vinyl, which wipes clean of spills with the whisk of a damp cloth. There are matching silvery flats if the hostesses wish. Hostesses may style their hair as they choose, so long as it is neat in appearance. And if the girls like, they may wear earrings of their own choosing – so long as the earrings are small, button style and in gold or silver. Braniff's hostess look is chic feminine. Is simplicity and comfort and individual. It's color, it's fashion and just as in 1965 is setting the new trend in airline fashions – elegance.' Braniff babes soon earned their own nickname, 'Puccis Galore', and the 'jet set' was born.

The Italian state airline, Alitalia, did not have stewardesses until as late as the 1950s – until then, on board the 22-seater Alitalia Fiat 212 it had been difficult to offer even a hot drink (except for what could be contained in a Thermos flask) so there had been no need for them. By 1968, however, the fleet had been updated and Alitalia had commissioned uniforms from no less than the renowned Milanese fashion house Mila Schoen, who included among its many famous clients Marella Agnelli, wife of the president of Fiat and reputed to be one of the most elegant women in the world. For the first time the prêt-à-porter formula was applied to uniform design, mixing exclusivity with ready-to-wear practicality – Schoen's laboratory of high fashion used modern materials, crease-resistant for at least 18 months. The complete Alitalia stewardess's

RIGHT Japan Airlines
stewardesses dressed in navy
suits, c.1958, designed by
Mohei Ito. In 1960, Ito
shortened the skirt to just
above the knee and added
gold buttons.

ABOVE Serious business
pinstripes for the All Nippon
Airways stewardess, 1990s.

LEFT Japan Airlines' retro line-up, designed by, from right to left: 1951–54 Minoru Monta; 1954–60 and 1960–67 Mohei Ito; 1967–70, 1970–77 and 1977–87 Hanae Mori; and 1988–96 Shigenobu Motoi.

ABOVE Japan Airlines introduced the smart grey two-piece in 1951.

wardrobe comprised of a green suit in a wool material wearable in both winter and summer; a green woollen cape; a flight dress in washable material; a blue felt hat, and shoes and boots in finest blue leather made specially for Alitalia by Magli of Bologna. (The new uniforms were modelled for the press photographs by Barbara Bach, a little-known model, later to become a Bond girl and Mrs Ringo Starr.) As well as designing what Schoen described as a 'graceful and young look currently fashionable,' he created a uniform which coped with all kinds of movement while retaining the line and shape of the cut. As the Alitalia publicity department of the time put it, 'The line of the outfit, the grace with which it is worn, the vivacity of the colours create a picture of the company which passengers of every nationality can identify: what the English call "image".'

The airline industry was predominantly male-orientated; chauvinism reigned. Fashion initiatives, such as those introduced by Braniff and Alitalia, reinforced the notion that the aircraft's aisle was something of a stewardess's catwalk in the air, largely for the benefit of the male travellers, not to mention the occupants of the cockpit. In the late 1960s and early 1970s, art imitated life or perhaps it was the other way round, as film screenplays of the time created stereotypes of heart-throb captains and swooning stewardess characters. In real life, dozens of captains and first-officers married stewardesses and dozens of jet-setting, high-powered businessmen plucked trophy wives from the ranks of the stewardess legions. The airline industry opportunis-

Hat attack:

FACING BOTTOM Lufthansa's flying crane logo adorned the caps of the airline's stewardesses in 1955.

FACING TOP LEFT Felicity Downer modelled the British United Airways' uniform for the new season in 1967.

FACING TOP RIGHT The first UK-based non-white stewardesses to be employed by an independent airline received their 'wings' at the London offices of British Midland Airways in 1970. From left: Innez Matthews, Irma Reid and Cindy Medford.

ABOVE Florida-based National Airlines introduced a new uniform in 1971. It evolved from a list of design features suggested by stewardesses themselves. Modelled by, from left, Janet Heinz, Wisty Mixon and Cynthia Robertson. (See p41.)

ABOVE In stark contrast to the propriety (often to the point of prudishness) shown by most airlines to that date, in 1973 Southwest Airlines threw caution to the winds with its stewardess uniform. 'The girls must be able to wear kinky leather boots and hot pants or they don't get the job,' said the airline's *male* bosses.

ABOVE RIGHT Wearing their new uniforms designed by Pierre Balmain, a group of TWA stewardesses wave in unison on the Place de la Concorde. The girls had just received their diplomas during a ceremony held at a Paris hotel, 1965.

FACING Janet Jackson, a stewardess for American Airlines, is seen here modelling a miniskirted uniform in 1965. Janet wore the outfit around Nashville Airport to test public reaction to the new garb.

tically lapped up the sex theme and served it to their clients. Southwest Airlines of Texas admitted that 'sex sells seats' and to prove it clad their stewardesses in thigh-exposing hot pants and knee-high, brilliant-white leather 'kinky' boots. Across the Pacific and Atlantic, other airlines followed suit: Greek designer Yannia Tseklenis created a white-boots-and-flared-trouser-suit combination, set off with a gold chain-link belt for her homeland's national airline, Olympic Airways. Pierre Cardin and Pierre Balmain designed new uniforms for Pakistan International Airways and TWA respectively; Jean Louis designed for United, Bill Blass for American, Ralph Lauren for TWA, Roland Klein for BOAC and Sir Hardy Amies for BOAC and BEA.

Amies' ethos made him the perfect choice to design for Britain's national airlines – he was a self-confessed snob. (Of the new, classless society, he said, 'Total rubbish. If a society has no class, it's not a society.') Amies was known principally as one of London's foremost couturiers and as a menswear consultant on a worldwide scale. The House of Hardy Amies had experience in coping with the restraints of designing for the mass market, having worked for the British Airports Authority, the British Police Force, the South African Army, Navy and Air Force, and many others. The unveiling of the new 1972 BEA uniform followed months of research, during which more than 400 girls (as female air crew were referred to in the 1970s) were consulted. 'Fly the flag', was the patriotic message. The emphasis, said Hardy Amies, was on self-expression. 'I want to make the girls look lady-like and elegant. There is a strong current trend away from unifor-

mity, especially among the young, so I have designed a uniform which does allow the expression of individuality. This is achieved by the use of interchangeable colours based on strong red, white and blue. Perhaps the most inspiring thing about the whole project has been the interest shown by the girls themselves. No designer can work in a vacuum and the hundreds of girls we spoke to left us in no doubt about the kind of clothes they wanted.' Dresses, blouses and overalls were issued in various colourways so that the crew could dress according to their mood. The French blue 22-ounce wool worsted overcoat, the 18-ounce wool worsted jacket and dress with contrasting red stitching and centre back zip fastening and a choice of Breton-style or Tutankhamen-style hats met with approval: 'All women like getting new clothes and the new uniform really does look and feel lovely,' commented Mo Mullan, Chief Stewardess.

Redesigns of uniforms on a two-year cycle almost became the norm, following fashion, colour-ways and hemlines. In a business in which standards of service and even fare pricing were regulated, image became the distinguishing factor between airlines, and air stewardesses were in the front line. Stewardesses were selected for their looks as much as for their ability, and some companies even had compulsory resignation policies (or transfer to ground work) after the age of 25 or 30, or if the young woman married. The image of the air stewardess epitomized the excitement of travel for a whole generation of young women in the 1960s and 70s whose options had previously been to become either secretaries or shop assistants. Air stewardesses

TOP LEFT **Lufthansa's summer collection, 1955–65.**
TOP RIGHT **Icelandic Air stewardesses pose with a model Douglas DC-8, 1960s.**

ABOVE **BEA's popular uniforms, designed by Sir Hardy Amies, 1972.**
FACING **BEA's classic tailoring, 1960.**

Braniff International's advertising and marketing expert, Mary Wells employed Italian fashion designer Emilio Pucci to create stunning outfits that broke the popular formula of uniform design (see p22).

FACING 'Braniff Babes', as they were known, are seen here modelling Pucci's 1966 uniforms on board a full-size model of the Boeing SST (supersonic transport). The SST was Boeing's answer to Concorde, but never got off the ground.

ABOVE Pucci's bubble helmet was used in the days prior to the air-bridge to protect the coiffure from wind and rain on the walk from the terminal to the aircraft. A Braniff International stewardess models the plexiglass headgear at John F. Kennedy Airport, New York in 1965.

were seen as almost equal to models or rock stars in the glamour stakes. The stewardess was now clearly recognized and implemented as an intrinsic part of the corporate identity by most of the international airlines.

In 1993, a facsimile of the world's best-known stewardess – The Singapore Girl – was unveiled at Madame Tussaud's waxworks museum in London, the first commercial figure to be displayed at the museum. Madame Tussaud's said the figure was chosen 'to reflect the ever-growing popularity of international travel'. The Singapore Girl is the embodiment of the successful marketing concept and is one of the airline industry's most instantly recognized figures. She is a global marketing icon and probably one of the most important elements of Singapore Airlines' (SIA) corporate identity. In her distinctive uniform, a sarong kebaya in batik material designed by Parisian couturier Pierre Balmain, she personifies what SIA describes as the 'tradition of friendly service and Asian hospitality.' Around 85 per cent of all Singapore Girls are either Singaporean or Malaysian. The remainder, most of whom are recruited for their language skills, are from China, India, Indonesia, Japan, Korea and Taiwan. Created in 1972, when Singapore Airlines was formed (following the division of the former Malaysia-Singapore Airlines into two carriers – Malaysian Airline System and SIA) – she has spearheaded SIA's international marketing and advertising campaigns ever since.

FACING Greek designer, Yannia Tseklenis created a casual 'new look' for her national airline, Olympic Airways, using the Olympic rings motif in a variety of imaginative ways in 1971.

ABOVE LEFT Denim Air – the ultimately casual look in the 1980s.

ABOVE Mary Quant echoed the colours of Court Line Aviation's livery for her uniform design. A camel coloured overcoat or jacket was worn over a cotton blouse in bright pink, magenta, orange or turquoise. A pink denim apron was worn for cabin service. The uniforms were modelled by Anne, Claire, Jenny and Lorraine at Luton Airport, UK in 1973.

LEFT Germany's budget airline LTU commemorated 40 years of service in the 1980s by publishing photographs of its uniforms past and present. An annual redesign is shown here, from left – 1968,1969 and 1970.

British Airways, like so many other big airlines, has revised and updated its uniforms many times. Often the airlines are trying to make more than just one fashion statement: 'we're friendly', 'we're reliable' and, of course, 'we're (at least a little bit) sexy' all vie for attention.

LEFT & ABOVE RIGHT British Airways uniforms, designed by Roland Klein in 1985, included a silk-look polyester jacquard tunic with blue leather belt and midnight blue blazer. And plenty of platinum braid for the flight crew.

RIGHT Audrey Meston modelled the well-cut lines of the uniform designed by Paul Costelloe in 1994.

For Balmain and others, the national costume was a prerequisite element of the brief from the airline and also a source of inspiration for the designer who was progressively trying to get away from the military-style uniform. The Eastern charm of the Air-India stewardess was successfully linked to the Taj Mahalian decor of both the interior and exterior of Air-India's fleet of 'Jumbo Jets'. In reaction to the increasingly international mix of passenger traffic, Japanese kimonos and Japanese smiles were apparent on the Lufthansa Far East route from Frankfurt to Tokyo. Working within religious and social constraints, the Balenciaga Fashion House's designs for the Middle-Eastern airline Gulf Air attempted to mix a Western trouser-suit and an Arab headdress. Gulf Air's 'generations' of uniforms have ranged from early flowing haremesque peach to navy blue business-style.

On the other side of the planet, national costume was not part of the brief or creative influence for Florida-based National Airlines as it launched its new uniform on the non-stop daily flight from Miami to London. 'Uniforms that purr' were to be worn by all National's 1,000 stewardesses. The topcoat was of simulated tigerskin with a full-notched collar and six double rows of buttons, and there was a 'tigerskin' hat to match. The uniform had been formulated from a list of design features suggested by National stewardesses themselves – an interesting departure from the traditional hire-a-famous-fashion-designer concept.

FACING A cool and casual look for SAS in 1999: a quasi-baseball cap for the stewardess and a pair of chinos for the steward were combined with the authority of metal cap badges and buttons.

ABOVE Classic uniforms in olive green and dark blue were designed by Giorgio Armani for Alitalia in the 1990s.

ABOVE LEFT Pan American's ground staff were given a style overhaul by American designer Anne Klein in 1970. Modelled here by Sally Stone, the uniform was a combination of jolly plaid pants and cosy, practical polo neck sweater, giving out a message with something of a 'fun mom' about it.

LEFT Virgin Atlantic Airways' £3 million design revamp created by John Rocha for the company's 5,000 employees included uniforms for on-board beauty therapists as well as stewardesses, pictured here with Virgin's chief, Sir Richard Branson. Bright, in-your-face red was the company's trademark.

Thai International Airlines followed the Western fashion for business-suit-type uniforms in the 1950s (ABOVE) and 70s (ABOVE LEFT), only varying colours and fabrics. By the 1990s, however, the airline was tapping into celebrating national and cultural heritage in its attire, at least in part (LEFT).

With the arrival of the Boeing 747 'Jumbo Jets' in the late 1960s, the whole world of aviation changed. Mass transport replaced exclusivity (with the exception of first and business class). Even though crew/passenger ratios were increased to cope with the demand, the stewardess became an airborne waitress in a busy café – and consequently sometimes condescendingly referred to as the 'trolley dolly'. The impetuous creativity of the 1960s was quelled and the rise of feminism (and regulations) forced companies to drop discriminatory policies and allow older crew to stay airborne. Competition, as a result of deregulation, and the fuel crisis took their toll on the airlines. Braniff, for all its style, was one of the first casualties. Company cutbacks meant that the tired businessman was joined in the coach seats by the holidaying family and the roaming backpacker. The emphasis shifted to safety and security; 'trust us', as important a message as 'enjoy us'. This, too, was reflected in the design of uniforms, which emphasized practicality and smartness. Glamour was beginning to wane. Bright and happy holidaymaking was now available to the masses and in 1973 Britain's biggest holiday airline, Court Line Aviation, showed off its colourful new uniforms at Luton Airport. Mary Quant's design consisted of a bright cotton blouse in pink, magenta, orange or turquoise, echoing the colours of Court Line's aircraft livery. A striped cravat was worn with the suit along with a camel-coloured knitted waistcoat; tan shoes or knee length boots were the options for the feet and the ensemble was topped off by a camel-coloured hat. A pink denim apron was worn for cabin service.

FACING Middle East meets West in the 1970s with Gulf Air's adaptation of the Muslim headdress; legs are covered by smart trousers.

ABOVE The headdress remains in the 1990s redesign by the Balenciaga Fashion House, as do those ubiquitous smiles.

In contrast to the ebullient creativity of the 1960s and early 1970s, and reflecting the terrestrial fashion styles, TWA launched Ralph Lauren's military-inspired, retro-styled uniforms in 1978. Lauren, known for his impeccably tailored classics, dressed the flight attendants in navy wool for fall/winter and grey-blue wool for spring/summer, a return to 'traditional, clean-cut styles that put a touch of "uniform" back in the uniforms,' as described in the TWA press release. Thus began the path toward the sensible two-piece as worn by the commuting corporate set.

With renewed interest in business and first-class travel for both the flying public and the airlines in the 1980s and 90s, uniforms took on the business suit guise. Hi-tech materials of stretchy wool textiles for summer and winter jackets, skirts and trousers ensured ease of movement and comfort. Giacomo and Mirella Bizzini's leading Italian fashion manufacturer, The Nadini Group, produced the Mondrian line for Alitalia in 1998 (replacing uniforms by Giorgio Armani). 'The Mondrian product line,' said Mirella Bizzini, 'is intended for women who are willing to keep their own identity and fail to mingle with the crowd, while abstaining from showing off. Our uniform is based on such criteria and actually deserves to be termed a "travel suit", given its wearability, comfort and innovation.'

Virgin Atlantic Airways' £3 million uniform overhaul for 'the new millennium' was created by international award-winning designer John Rocha and was designed to provide 'an elegant

LEFT Stewardess Aban Mistry models the Air-India uniform next to the Taj Mahalian decor of an Air-India 'Jumbo Jet', 1971. The short salwar-kameez was both culturally appropriate and practical for serving in the cabin. The elegant dupatta scarf added an extra flourish.

ABOVE The marketing icon of SIA, the Singapore Girl (see p36): the colourful sarong kebaya uniforms were first designed by Pierre Balmain in 1968.

RIGHT The first Singapore Girl, pictured with a traffic officer, 1947; the uniform was entirely Western in style.

look' that brought back 'the romance into flying with a contemporary edge'. He clad the new female cabin crew in red and gave the male crew members a contrasting three-piece charcoal grey suit. The design echoed the 1978 TWA/Ralph Lauren approach of retrospective influence – the tried-and-tested never fails but doesn't necessarily inspire either.

There seems little innovation in uniform design since the bravado of Emilio Pucci in the 1960s and the elegance of Balmain for SIA. It would be interesting to see how Alexander McQueen, Vivienne Westwood or Jean-Paul Gaultier might clothe the cabin crew operatives in the 21st century. Thankfully, 1950s science-fiction fanzine writers' predictions of 21st-century uniforms with nylon leggings for both sexes and metallic jerkins featuring enormous winged epaulets have not been taken on board, but there may be a missed opportunity for airlines to be adventurous and re-establish their brand with truly innovative fashion design. Although the real glamour days for stewardesses are now in the past, the profession will probably never lose its aura of romanticism and authority. With the aid of a uniform, a mere look from a stewardess can still make a grown man (or woman) sit down and belt up.

food

In the early 1920s, in-flight refreshment on board a converted Handley Page bomber consisted of a thermos flask of coffee and, for an extra three shillings, a lunch box containing a sandwich, fruit and chocolate. By the late 1920s, Lufthansa became the first airline to provide hot meals on its Berlin-to-Vienna express route. On board the *Rayon d'Or* (Golden Ray) route from Paris to London in the 1930s, Air Union (now Air France) served de luxe cuisine on fine bone china. Tables were laid with starched crisp, white linen, cut crystal glasses and a vase of fresh flowers. Now, the award-winning 'cheferati' command healthy consultancy fees for planning in-flight menus and vintners suggest suitable bottles of Chardonnay with which to wash down the ragout and roasted root vegetables. However, it is not all Bacchanalia in the skies – some short-haul routes offer the passenger nothing more than a chilled-to-tasteless roll and a well-known brand of chocolate bar.

Today, the inflight and travel catering industry is more about logistics than about cooking. The industry is now worth over 40 billion US dollars and is represented by two official associations – the International Flight Catering Association and the International Inflight Food Service Association. Conferences, seminars and trading events on a global scale are staged, culminating in two, three-day Oscar-style award ceremonies. The associations are also involved in lobbying local and international governments on legislative matters on behalf of the industry. The big players in the industry are LSG Skychefs (Lufthansa Services Group) with around 220 locations worldwide and 41,000 staff, and Gate Gourmet (originally a merger of two Swissair companies) with 142 locations

Spam and other assorted cold meats are accompanied by tinned vegetables and fresh fruit on board a BOAC Sunderland flying-boat bound for India from Hythe in the port of Southampton, UK, 1945.

in 27 countries and 26,000 staff. Other independents include Servair and Alpha Flight Services – the latter is the UK's top airline caterer and satisfies over forty million appetites per year. From one base at Heathrow Airport, Alpha Flight Services can produce in excess of 20,000 meals per day.

The typical airline catering facility occupies thousands of square feet and houses flight kitchens, bond and warehouse space. As well as the main food preparation areas, test kitchens not only create new delights for ever-changing palates, but also test new cooking, chilling and storage machinery. Throughout the ergonomically designed site, food-freshness is key and stringent hygiene is paramount. Hygiene checks are carried out with temperature probes, hand-held implements called Biotraces which check for bacteria on work surfaces and constant laboratory analysis feedback. After preparation, food is blast-chilled to below 5 degrees celsius. Meals can then be stored for up to 12 hours before transit to the aircraft in specially manufactured trucks. Once on the aircraft, the cabin crew take over and re-heat the food in convection ovens to a minimum 145 degrees celsius.

The original airline caterers of the 1920s and 30s were hotels. For example, when it took up to two weeks to get from Hythe, near Southampton, UK to Sydney, Australia, on board a Short Bros. Empire flying-boat, most meals were served on the ground. (There was, however, a kitchen on board just to make sure appetites were always sated.) Passengers would alight and be driven or

FACING In the preparation kitchen at London Airport in the late 1940s, Catering Officer Stanley Jeanmond puts the finishing touches to an 'Elizabethan' meal for consumption on the BOAC 'Elizabethan' service, watched by Chef Stinton, left, and Chef Keel.

LEFT Mayonnaise with everything in the airport kitchens of the 1970s.

ABOVE The photographer took 6½ hours to set up the 38,000 items required to service the appetites on board a British Airways Boeing 747.

ABOVE Healthy vittles served by
KLM (Royal Dutch Airlines),
1920s.

RIGHT Lufthansa's first class in-
flight service en route from
Berlin to Vienna, 1928.

FACING Checking the 'wurst' for
firmness and the baskets of
provisions prior to take-off,
KLM, 1920s.

walked to a nearby hotel where they would be gastronomically 'refuelled' while the aircraft would be literally refuelled and essential maintenance carried out.

Airline chefs used to come from hotel and restaurant backgrounds. In America, Jim Marriott, of the Marriott Hotels Group, started one of the first inflight catering services, Marriott Corporation, which flourished in the 1940s and 50s and has since become Cater Air and subsequently LSG Sky-chefs. While big-name terra firma chefs such as Anton Mosimann for British Airways and Raymond Blanc for Virgin may be weighty assets in marketing terms and are doubtless useful as advisors, the real airline industry chefs are highly trained and very specialized professionals. The reality of airline catering is that portion control is one of the most important factors when preparing millions of meals per year. When a five star restaurant executive chef marks-up the cost of a meal by 200 or 300 per cent then portion control can afford to be flexible; however, when an airline meal recipe specifies 30 grammes of chopped shallots per head multiplied by 30,000 passengers for the north Atlantic routes, for example, there is no room within the profit margins to be cavalier with the portions.

There are significant variations in the airlines' attitudes to portion control. Some airlines have very strict directives for the catering companies. American Airlines uses AirServe, a computer-generated monthly catering manual with precise portion controls and very exacting instructions,

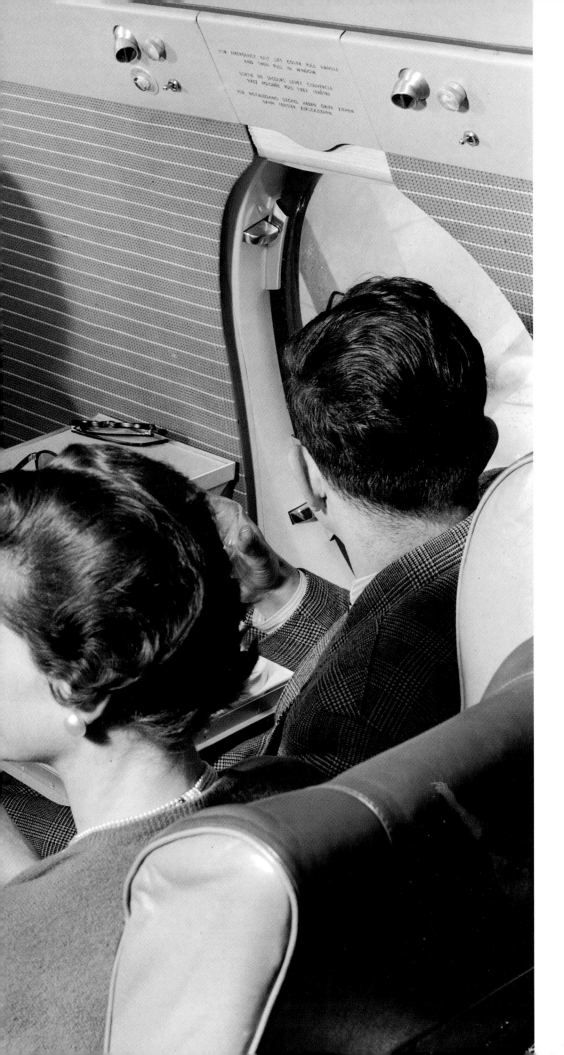

LEFT Lunch in first class on board a BEA Vickers Viscount, 1953. Flying was still a luxurious mode of transport, with space for congenial eating and seating arrangements; one could also enjoy an after-dinner smoke.

ABOVE Glass tumbler, 1960s.

LEFT Bacchanalian motifs served as a backdrop to cocktail hour on Lufthansa's first class 'Senator' service, 1958.

ABOVE Lufthansa's rose remains a symbol of high-quality service to this day.

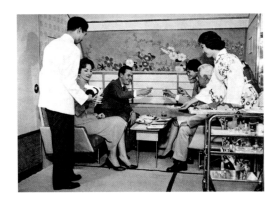

LEFT Essential ice provisions are loaded on board to complement 'The Real Thing', 1930s.

TOP First class service included saki and smiles on board a Vickers Super VC10 flight from Tokyo to London, 1964.

ABOVE Champagne and sushi in the 'Kiku-no-ma' lounge of a Japan Airlines Douglas DC-8 in the 1950s. The Kiku (chrysan-themum) is the imperial flower of Japan.

right down to the size of knife to be used when preparing a 35 x 4mm julienne of vegetables for a main course. There is a code number for each recipe and directions: 'trim the ends, cut the onion in half, refrigerate until needed'. The airline's regional catering managers police the end product. Other airlines are not so particular and leave the formula up to the catering service company who will present a menu from a brief which is always based on cost.

The problem with the strict AirServe directions is that there is little room for regional variation; a midwest American chef's perception of Tagliatelle Carbonara may not be authentic to a fifth gen-eration Sicilian, so, when a Boeing takes off from Las Vegas for Rome with 50 per cent of the passengers being Italian, disappointment sets in. The equation is, however, difficult to balance: an American pizza with its half-inch-thick base and bucket of topping may suit the oil executive from Texas but not the couturier from Milan.

Cross-border diet requirements vary enormously. Today there are fairly universal eating habits on most airlines and those habits have changed considerably over the years. The reason for change is that the passenger profile has changed. A high percentage of BOAC customers in the 1950s to 70s were Anglo-Saxon Christians, so pork chops and roast beef were menu favourites. In first class on the Boeing 747, a sanguine topside of beef would be carved on the trolley in front of the salivating passenger. Now, the clientele can be Hindu, Hebrew, Shamanist, Muslim and agnostic vegan.

Standards of cuisine can be extremely high – for those paying for the privilege at any rate. Singapore Airlines, for example, boasts The Singapore Airlines International Culinary Panel with award-winning chefs from the USA, Hong Kong, Japan, Australia, India and France. Such delights on offer are an hors d'oeuvre of Premium Chilled Malossal Caviar followed by Baked Barramundi Fillet in Banana Leaf with Linguini, Shiitake Mushrooms and Arugula or Chicken and Prawns in a Paper Bag with Oriental Seasonings – all included in the price of a first-class ticket. In economy class, however, higher volume and lower unit cost means less passenger choice and – due to the multi-part process of blast chill, freeze and re-heat – foods that work well on board are 'wet' meals such as stews and sauces; Indian food is particularly suitable.

People's eating styles are changing and there is now more of a 'grazing' culture. Passengers do not want to be told when to have a meal, but would rather either go to sleep, read the newspaper or check for emails on the laptop. Reflecting social and cultural trends on the ground – freedom of choice for the individual – British Airways has developed a concept called 'Raid the Larder'. A bar is available for business-class passengers to prepare their own plates from a selection of breads and cheeses etc. As usual, economy passengers may have to wait for this service to filter toward the rear of the aircraft.

ABOVE LEFT Champagne and silver service in first class on board a Lufthansa Boeing 707, 1960s.

TOP 1970s style: food, fashion and glassware in first class on an American Airlines DC-10, 1976.

LEFT A passenger has ordered a glass of cider and the bar steward happily complies, Lufthansa, 1960.

ABOVE Lobster and caviar flank Lebanese mezze served by a Gulf Air steward, 1980s.

Due to sociological changes in eating and drinking habits, galleys on board Concorde have been restyled. The Concorde passenger of the 1970s ate steak and drank malt whisky. Today, we know that litres of water stave off dehydration and should one want to imbibe, a chilled Mâcon Villages or vintage Krug is a relatively healthier alternative. Therefore, more liquid has to be carried, which means more weight, which means more fuel, which means lower profits. With this in mind and using new, lighter technologies such as microwave and fan ovens, London-based product design consultancy Factory redesigned the Concorde galleys using a modular system to more readily take into account changes in eating habits now and over the next decade.

When it comes to wine, can anyone appreciate the finer bouquets of 'strawberry', 'boiling tar' and 'summer meadows' in a pressurized cabin at eight miles high? The pressurization does affect taste, but the main problem is dehydration. After the first hour or so in the air, nostrils dry out and olfactory senses are nullified. Dehydration can also accentuate certain elements such as tannin and acidity, so a good quality claret can taste fine on the ground but not at 35,000 feet. In economy class, the problem is compounded further by plastic beakers which suppress any qualities a wine may have.

In the battle for recognition and individuality, airlines created their own unique 'services'. In the days before 'political correctness', some American businessmen in the 1950s were pampered with

FACING TOP **Virgin Atlantic Airways' minimalist first class place setting, late 1990s.**

FACING **Extra payload of heavy ceramics offered to Lufthansa's first class passengers, 1973. The small rotund earthenware pot contained pickled herrings.**

ABOVE **Delftware miniatures of Dutch houses containing Bols gin were presented as gifts to KLM first class passengers.**

BELOW **Qantas Empire Airways' coffee cup, late 1930s.**

FACING TOP By the 1990s the emphasis on food in first class cabins was more on quality than quantity, as indicated by the dishes of delicacies served on Thai International Airlines.

FACING BOTTOM 1980s first class non-vegetarian diet from British Airways.

ABOVE Meals on long-haul economy flights have always been carefully measured out as this All Nippon Airways tray of small compartments demonstrates.

LEFT The bijou aesthetics – and portion control – of chef Anton Mosimann for British Airways.

THIS PAGE Fresh from Tokyo's Tsukiji fish market, in 2000 All Nippon Airways offers sushi and sashimi washed down with saki and miso soup in Club Class.

OVERLEAF LEFT Sunday roast every day of the week: first class BOAC VC10, 1964.

OVERLEAF RIGHT Hyperactive diet: fast food for children in the 1950s and the 1980s.

cocktails and cigars on internal 'Men-Only' flights. In the 1960s, Continental Airlines featured a 'Pink Buffet' service for first class passengers offering hors d'oeuvres, fruits, cheeses and complimentary champagne. Corporate image was and is a very important tool and just as airlines have developed their own unique livery outside the aircraft, they have also desired their own unique style inside. Identity consultancies offer a product design service to create distinctive cutlery and crockery shapes. There is a move away from square plastic, get-as-many-dishes-on-a-tray culture to more organic, oval shapes that are inspired by elements of either the corporate identity or national heritage. The display of the logo on crockery is becoming more subliminal for aesthetic reasons but also because there is evidence that an airline-branded item has more trophy-status and is more likely to be stolen. Characteristically, Virgin Airways took advantage of the petty pilfering by printing 'Stolen from Virgin Airways' on the base of its jocund, aeroplane-shaped cruet set.

In the highly competitive market of commercial aviation, food and drink is one of the most important attractions for the passenger. When boredom and discomfort set in, the chance to unpack the cutlery and sample the fayre is a welcome distraction. Back on the ground, airline food is a popular subject among the recently disembarked clientele and if the refreshments are poor the message gets passed on – a good enough reason to choose an alternative airline for the next trip. Conversely, if the food is appreciated then recommendations ensue. Certainly eating is one of the essentials of life but in the air it is much more about entertainment.

interiors

As a schoolboy in the mid-1960s, I sat behind the bulkhead on a Comet IV on my way to the Middle East. I remember wondering who was responsible for designing the wallpaper. The padded panel depicted the history of flight from the Montgolfier brothers to the first commercial aircraft – it was the last thing you wanted to look at as you reached for the bile-green sick bag. By 1972, terrestrial interior design trends were in full flight: flame retardant fabrics in mustard, orange and pea-green adorned the walls, floors and furniture of aircraft. Bold, swirling patterns on some airlines were the perfect emetic for the delicate stomach. Today, smoother, quieter aircraft and smoother, quieter interiors help maintain an equilibrium. Some airlines today are the epitome of comfort: Singapore Airlines, for example, boasts, 'Luxurious seats, upholstered in the finest Connolly leather and rich wood trimmings, [which] recline to any angle desired – offering the ultimate night-time retreat, they also transform into inviting beds with a soft, comfortable mattress and a down-filled duvet.'

Things were different back in the 1920s, aboard the converted First World War Handley Page 0/400 bi-plane bomber, where the chair was fashioned from wicker and sparsely padded with kapok and leatherette – it resembled a luxury cat basket and offered as much protection. Handley Page's publicity leaflet explained the arrangement of the accommodation: 'after-cabin to seat six, forward-cabin to seat two passengers, and for those who prefer to travel in the open, two seats are arranged in front of the pilot. An observation platform with a sliding roof is fitted in the

FACING **Stairway to heaven: in the days before fuel crises and subsequent policies of maximizing passenger count per square metre, the upper deck of the Boeing 747 housed a cocktail lounge, while space under the stairs served as a drinks cabinet,1970.**

ABOVE **Early in-flight entertainment on board a Handley Page: a hand-cranked projector screens the first film ever shown on a commercial aircraft, 1925.**

The Boeing 747 first-class 'Tiger Lounge' bar. Built as a mock-up in 1972 for a Boeing product-development study, the lounge for first- and business-class passengers was to be situated in the hold with a vertical viewing port in the central table.

IMPERIAL
AIRWAYS
MAP
CALCUTTA — SYDNEY

The most luxurious Flying-Boat in the world

Length 88ft. 6ins. • Height on water line 24ft. • Speed 200 M.P.H. (Approx.)
Span 114 feet • Weight fully loaded 18 tons • Crew 5 Accommodation 24 passengers
on day stages and 16 on night journeys
'The Empire Flying-Boat'-28 are now being built by

IMPERIAL AIRWAYS

after-cabin.' The converted bombers, however, had an air of luxury with curtains at the windows and a basket of flowers between the pairs of seats.

In the post-First World War competition to lure passengers into the skies, many airlines fitted out their cabins with opulent luxury. The Deutsche Flugzeugwerke offered upholstered floors, walls, ceilings and seating, and the Dutch-designed and American-operated Fokker F-32 of 1930 introduced reclining seats in alligator skin, steward call buttons, reading lights and a lounge clad in walnut panelling and decorator fabrics. Despite the marketing hype and promise of comfort, however, the early flights were very noisy, bumpy and breezy. With the introduction of the Boeing 247 in 1933, though, the Americans changed the shape of airliners from the box-section to a more sleek, curved and aerodynamic fuselage, and the trend moved away from luxurious Pullman-like interiors towards simpler, more functional cabins. United Airlines ordered the new, all-metal Boeing 247 monoplane and cut trans-American flying times to under 20 hours. Sound-proofing, heating and air-conditioning were introduced, enabling audible conversation and allowing passengers to discard their heavy overcoats. In 1935, the Douglas Aircraft Company responded with the DC-3. With a cruising speed of 180mph, the resilient DC-3 carried twice as many passengers as the Boeing. The Douglas interior was also more comfortable, with a straight walk-through cabin; the Boeing 247 engineers had decided to run the main wing cross-spar through the cabin, above floor-level, so passengers had to high-step across the obstacle.

FACING The Empire flying-boat was the height of luxury and included a promenade deck to view the scenes below on the long stages to Africa, India and Australia, 1930s/40s.

ABOVE One of two 20-seat compartments on board an Imperial Airways 'Argosy'. The two compartments on the biplane were separated by a cocktail bar, 1930.

BELOW A surviving seat from a Handley Page 0/400 – a converted First World War bomber, 1919.

OVERLEAF LEFT Dressing room on a Hermes IV aircraft, 1950.

OVERLEAF RIGHT Dressing for dinner on board a BOAC Bristol Britannia, 1956.

With the introduction of the flying-boats in the mid-1930s, the possibilities of long-haul flight really took off. Britain's Government-backed Imperial Airways reduced travelling times to the territories of the Empire with the use of the Short Bros. C-class Empire flying-boat, followed by Pan American Airways who opened up the trans-Pacific and Atlantic routes with the Boeing 314 flying-boat. The interior space of the 'flying-dining-cars', as they were known, was vast in comparison with earlier commercial aircraft. On the 9-foot-high promenade deck of the Empire, binoculars were provided for passengers who wished to stretch their legs and make full use of the extra-large windows. Accommodation for 24 daytime passengers or 16 sleepers was available on the fore, midship and aft cabins. The crew of five navigated and piloted from the upper deck. Southampton to Melbourne took a speedy ten-and-a-half days, with stop-overs in first-class hotels included in the price of a ticket. Following the 'big is best' maxim, the Pan American Airways Boeing was larger, carrying 74 passengers and a crew of eight – physically it was the largest commercially viable aircraft to fly until the arrival of the 'Jumbo Jet' 30 years later. The interior was fitted out like a suite at the Waldorf. The Boeing 314 was equipped with sleeping berths for 40 and separate dressing rooms for men and women. There was also a bar next to the galley that serviced the dining room and a private de luxe cabin in the tail section which doubled as a honeymoon suite. The crew's sleeping quarters, rest room and flight controls were on the upper deck. The 314 could cruise at speeds of 175 mph for 3,500 miles without refuelling, and serviced the New York to London and San Francisco to Hong Kong routes.

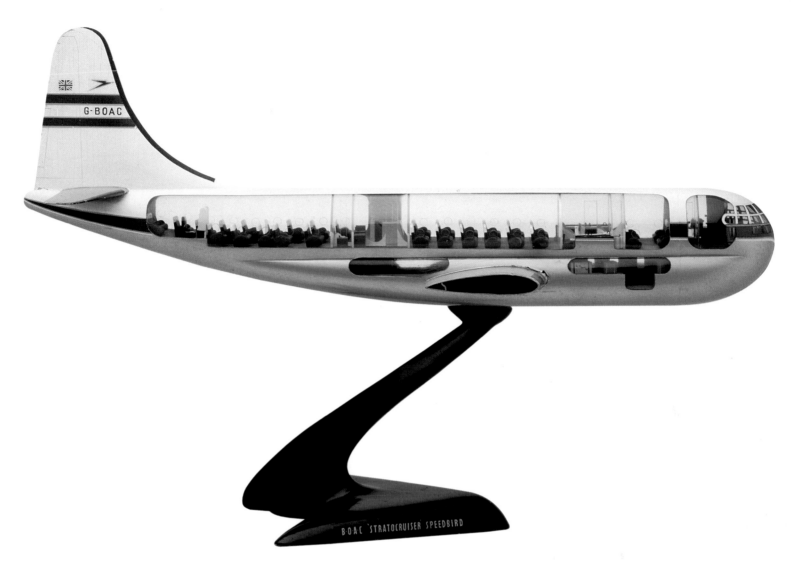

Corrosion from salt water, difficult maintenance issues and the hazard of floating detritus on landing and take-off were just some of the reasons why the flying-boat era didn't last. The Second World War led to the building of more landing strips and aerodromes around the globe and so 'land planes' took over as a more commercially viable form of air transport. After the war, resources in Europe were scarce and while Europeans made do with converted bombers as commercial aircraft, Americans enjoyed a healthy programme of aircraft and airline development. Douglas and Boeing were experienced companies and led the economic bonanza with a combination of higher speed planes and higher passenger payload. The record-breakingly-fast Douglas DC-6 had a pressurized cabin and so was able to climb above the clouds and bad weather to give passengers a much smoother ride.

The accelerated increase in the travel market led airlines and aircraft manufacturers to concentrate more on accommodating the passenger. By the late 1940s, new four-engined aircraft appeared, such as the double-decker Boeing Stratocruiser. The Stratocruiser featured sleeping berths and a capacity of 50 to 100 passengers, and leisurely flights allowed time to enjoy a four-course meal or a cocktail and a cigarette in the lower-deck lounge which was reached by a spiral staircase halfway down the main cabin. Seats had integral ashtrays, light switches, seat-reclining levers and stewardess call buttons. Larger overhead hand-luggage storage compartments had closable door fronts, as opposed to earlier open racks. Temperature was controlled by the bar

FACING The Boeing Stratocruiser offered accommodation on two decks; the lower one (bottom) offered an intimate environment for conversation.

TOP A wood and plastic travel agents' model shows the two decks and seating configuration on board the 'double-bubble' Stratocruiser.

ABOVE Hot chocolate and bedtime stories on board a Pan American Stratocruiser, 1949.

ABOVE Relaxing in a first-class
'Slumberette' on board a
Lockheed Constellation, early
1950s.

FAR RIGHT A TWA poster
advertises what the traveller
could expect to eat on board.

RIGHT A model of the
Constellation.

attendant and the desire to step outside for a breath of fresh air could be quasi-accomplished by the flick of a switch. A similarly advanced plane, the Lockheed Constellation, was so successful that Howard Hughes' TWA ordered a fleet straight from the drawing board in 1948.

By the early 1950s, Britain was back on track, revolutionizing speed and comfort with the smooth-flying, jet-propelled de Havilland Comet I. It put existing airliners in the shade due to its almost entire lack of vibration and the absence of noise. Henry Hensser wrote in his 1953 publication, *Comet Highway*: 'The limpid calm in the hull of the Comet is nothing short of a miracle. Eight miles above the earth and moving through the air at a speed of eight miles a minute ... A read, a smoke, a doze; quiet conversation; a coffee or a whisky-and-soda – the passenger takes his choice, for in this peaceful atmosphere all is conducive to relaxation.' The Comet I enjoyed only three years of service until a series of fatal accidents, due to metal fatigue, ended its career. However, the Comet IV, introduced in1958, was the first regular jet airliner service from London to New York.

Boeing introduced the hugely commercially successful 707, in the 1960s. The 707 jet opened up a new dimension in global travel – by 1965, in America alone, the annual air passenger count had doubled from that of 1958, to 100 million. Also in 1965, Braniff International Airways, adjusting to the tastes of all these extra travellers, revolutionized the interiors of their aircraft by hiring the talents of the designer Alexander Girard. 'Braniff advertised that the new look in travel was liter-

TOP **Proud parents look on as their son demonstrates smooth flying on board the jet-propelled de Havilland Comet IV, 1958.**

ABOVE **Exchanging her customary background of almond blossom, a Japanese lady poses in front of the silver contours of the Comet I air-intakes, 1953.**

ally taking off with its "flying colors" campaign,' wrote Lawrence Hughes in a 1966 article for *Air Transport World Supplement*. He went on to say, 'The ads described Girard as "busy redesigning our airplanes – in fact, tearing them apart ... he threw out nearly everything we had, and started from scratch".' In his overhaul of the aircraft interiors, Girard created seven different colour schemes and designed 56 different seat fabrics.

For all its speed and 'comfort', jet travel was boring – flying above the clouds meant views of cirrocumulus and perhaps another jet in the far distance, but little else. Airlines vied for attention and passengers in the 1970s encountered entertainment such as magicians pulling rabbits out of hats, Playboy bunnies and full-length feature films inside the cabin. (This was not the first time films had been shown on board – in 1925, a hand-cranked projector was used for the first time to entertain the full complement of six passengers on board a Handley Page.) Everything from piano bars to a choice of ten 'radio' channels with stereo-headphones became the norm. Meanwhile, the cabins of the jets got larger. The 'stretched' version of the successful Vickers VC10, for example, had space for 187 passengers in three seats each side of a central gangway, two galleys and seven toilets, plus one for the crew. Not all the increased space was what it seemed, however – lighting played an important part, not only in enlarging the interior space but also in creating different ambiences; the cabin crew could now control the mood of the passengers by changing the lighting from 'night time sleepy' to 'new day dawning' mode.

TOP Nightcap and slumbertime: with the introduction of Lufthansa's 'Senator' class in 1958, sections of the Lockheed Super Constellation were equipped with reclining seats.

LEFT Sleeping quarters on board a Sunderland flying-boat, 1947.

ABOVE Happy sleeping with American Airlines, 1970s.

ABOVE RIGHT On board a Singapore International Airlines Boeing 747, a passenger beds down with the helping hand of a Singapore Girl, 1977.

RIGHT Bedtime in first class, Qantas Airways, 1990s.

By the mid-1970s, with scheduled airlines carrying an estimated 500 million passengers per year, the need for real extra space was pressing. The Boeing 747 'Jumbo Jet' (which had been first introduced in 1969) was the answer to the ever-increasing population of air travellers, with its 20-foot-wide cabin, 8-foot-high ceiling, upper-deck lounge and almost 500-strong passenger capacity. There was plenty of room to walk up and down the twin aisles, and airlines and aircraft manufacturers used the space to entertain as well as accommodate. Boeing experimented with interiors by inviting potential passengers to try out mock-ups of 747 cabins as part of a product-development study. In 1972, Frank del Guidice designed the 'Tiger Lounge', intended for first-class and business-class passengers. The bright orange, deep-pile carpeted lounge was destined for the 747's windowless basement, potentially giving the world its first 3-storey commercial airliner. Large, fluorescent-lit panels and mirrored tiles set into carpeted wall and ceiling tiles gave an impression of daylight. In fact, the only window was a pretend 'tiger-skin' clad, central podium. The glass-topped podium doubled as a viewing port through the bottom of the aircraft. The 'Tiger Lounge', sadly, never left the development centre.

If the commercial airlines stopped short of the excesses of the 'Tiger Lounge', private jet owners in the 1970s went as far as they were able to produce opulent and seductive cabin interiors. When Hugh Hefner took delivery of his DC-9 jet from McDonnell Douglas in 1970, he named it 'Big Bunny' after his Playboy bunny girls, and decked the cabin with big leather seats, a video and a

Virgin Atlantic Airways' 1999 refurbishment of its aircraft included a new seat design with a built-in screen and a revamp of the beauty treatment area and bar in Upper Class.

stereo system. In a separate compartment, a large circular bed was covered in fur. Meanwhile, though stopping short of Hefner-type beds, Singapore Airlines, in a bid to improve comfort on their 747s, introduced an innovation for first-class passengers – the fully reclining swivel seat, dubbed the 'snoozzzer'. The 'snoozzzer' was fitted, in addition to the six 'slumberettes', on the upper deck.

Concorde, that unique delta-winged rocket that flies in inner space, has presented aircraft interior designers with the biggest challenges – having to satisfy the demands of some of the world's wealthiest customers within a decidedly cramped environment. Since the first scheduled flight in 1976, the British Airways' Concordes have each had three major interior facelifts. In 1998, the interior redesign commission was given to Factory, a London-based consultancy with a proven track record in designing transport interiors. They worked with Sir Terence Conran, whose team was responsible for the 'soft' side of the design work – the colour scheme, fabric design and cutlery design. The brief was not 'we need new seats and toilets', but a clean sheet of paper that invited ideas across the complete range of the customer experience. A bar area was proposed with a configuration that allowed reversible seating and tables to be installed on turn-around, thereby customizing the flight to suit the next passenger uptake. Other concepts to 'celebrate the theatre of Concorde,' as Factory director Adam White described it, included passenger viewing: a DVD relaying the first-hand responsibilities of the ground and flight crew who are wired with minia-

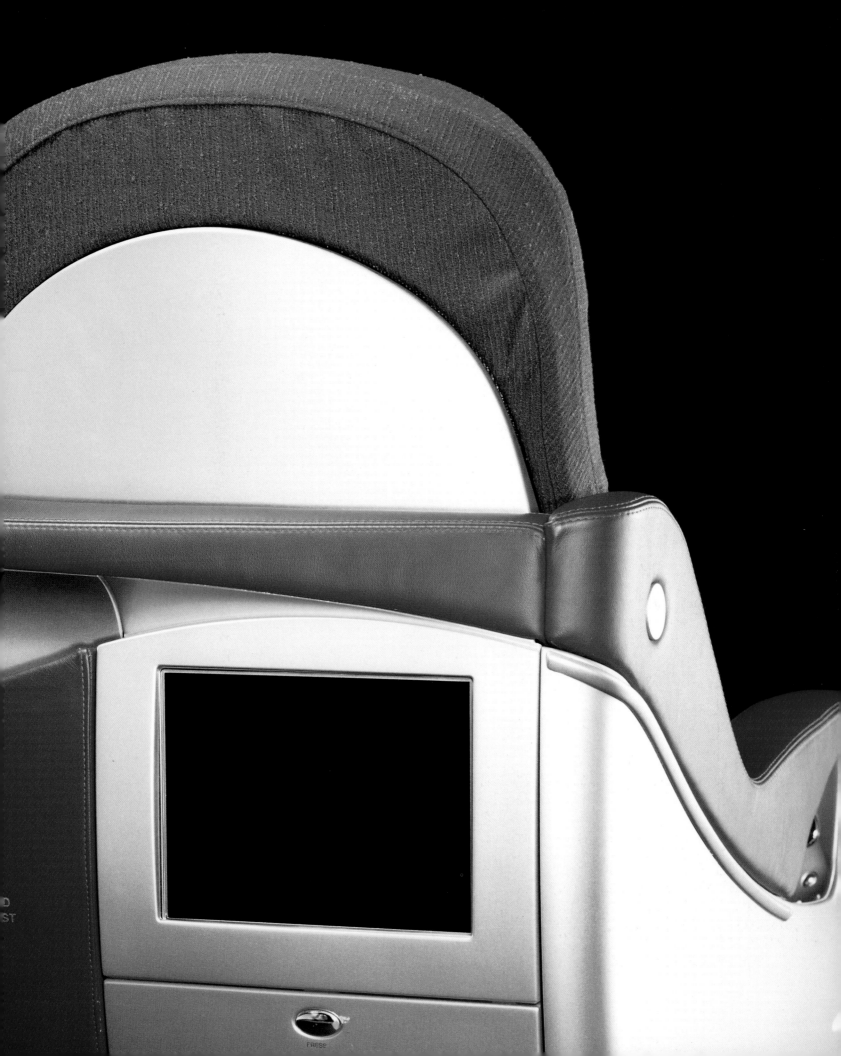

ture cameras; an updated cabin Machometer with displays mirroring those of the flight deck; and creating an awareness of the sensationless moment of breaking the sound barrier by passing a thin pulse of blue light down the inside length of the fuselage.

As mentioned, Concorde's personal space is restricted due to its relatively narrow fuselage. Factory's task was to design the seats cleverly as opposed to bigger. The availability of materials hadn't changed that much in the eight years since the previous seat was redesigned. The traditional airline seat has lots of moving parts in order to facilitate the reclining back, which is separate from the seat pad. There are also plenty of covering-up parts that hide the mechanism. The solution was a simple but innovative pivoting of the seat on a single point, leading to a more 'cupped' feeling without one's pelvis sliding down or underclothes riding up – phenomena that make regular long haul flying so uncomfortable. The added value of 20 to 30 per cent fewer parts meant fewer manufacturing problems.

The refurbished 'bathroom' (as it is tactfully referred to on Concorde) was stripped of its redundant waxed-paper cup and three-different-types-of-towel dispensers, in favour of a roomier, airier space. Four different light sources were created – main ambient, low-level floor, mirrored glass surfaces and low-level incandescent uplighters. The tiny warm-coloured uplighters were mounted in the basin shelf, giving the user a healthier appearance than normally allowed for

Entertainment in the early 21st century contrasts with early flight in the late 1920s when passengers listened to a wind-up gramophone and enjoyed the opportunity of a round of whist on Imperial Airways.

The interior of the private DC-9 as decked out for Playboy's chief, Hugh Hefner. He took delivery of the jet from aircraft manufacturer McDonnell Douglas in January 1970 and dubbed the aircraft, 'Big Bunny'. Black leather abounds, as does the unashamed use of animal pelts for the bed spread.

with the usual high-mounted, poor colour-rendering fluorescents. The tricks with light and space suggest the luxury of an expensive metropolitan hotel closet.

Virgin Atlantic Airways' £37 million overhaul of its Upper Class service in 1999 featured a new cabin, the highlights of which were an innovative seat design using the latest technology to provide greater levels of comfort. 'The electronic seat offers a range of sitting positions from upright to a 180 degree full-length bed which gives passengers 6 feet 8 inches of space in which to stretch and sleep. The seat glides under the passenger seat in front and extends to 76 inches with a 4-inch footwell at the end to offer more space,' explains the Virgin press release; it goes on: 'Traditional airline-seat tracks are being replaced with sculptural chrome legs fixed to the cabin floor and a solid metal shell provides passenger privacy. The seat uses metallic silver and chrome, while automotive red leather and warm purple textured fabric reflect the romantic era of flying in the 1930s.'

As part of the redesign, Virgin was the first commercial passenger airline to offer double beds in the sky, with twin seats transforming into a double bed. Further changes to the Virgin cabin environment included an onboard bar which allowed more passengers to sit and relax and drink. Seven bar stools surrounded a streamlined bar with integral lighting. A new dedicated beauty treatment area was also created to provide more privacy for a shoulder and hand massage, plus

FACING Reminiscent of a soft-furnishings warehouse; the plushly executive-looking, yet somewhat homely, decor of a Boeing Business Jet, 1990s.

THIS PAGE The designer's budget: $2 million. The designer's brief: 'It should look really, really cool.' Marc Newson's design in 1999 for the anonymously-owned $42 million Falcon 900B features padded-leather sofas that pull out to form a double bed, lacquer cabinetry, an entertainment system, space-age seating in black and silver leather and a hand-woven silk carpet. Newson collaborated with graphic designer Richard Allan to decorate the exterior with 'a giant dot screen'.

Airbus' huge A3XX double-decker will carry up to 600 passengers. The lower deck may house cafés, meeting rooms, gyms and sleeping cabins.

a wider range of beauty treatments. Virgin's economy cabins also benefited from the revamp, albeit in a mostly cosmetic way. New seat colours were introduced – orange, gold, red and vivid blue – with blankets and carpets to match. The updated 'amenity kit' was filled with added extras, such as earplugs, breath-freshening mints, lip balm and, rather oddly, a rubber duck named Lewis.

Developing new interiors can be an expensive business for an airline, but not as expensive as developing a new aircraft. The new double-decker, super-Jumbo Airbus A3XX is estimated to cost more than £8 billion before the first order is delivered. However, with a passenger capacity of 500 to 600 and a range of 14,000 kilometres, in cost-per-seat terms, the A3XX will be at least 15 per cent cheaper to run than the Boeing 747. There will be enough space beneath the passenger deck for cafés, meeting rooms, gyms, extra toilets and sleeping cabins. The cabin's layout is to be more flexible; in the early 1970s, cabins were refitted every ten years; now they are redone after four. Airbus's designers have minimized rigid fixtures, like galleys and toilets, so airlines can customize their A3XX cabins more quickly and cheaply. The storage areas are also being redesigned. During market research for the A3XX, one of the main complaints from passengers was lost luggage or the wait at luggage reclaim. Airbus may create special holds in first and business class, so passengers with a couple of bags can hand them to the stewards before take-off, then collect them on landing.

As part of British Airways' £200 million-plus Club World class overhaul, design group Tangerine's forward/rearward seating configuration transformed the traditional business-class cabin. The reclining chair and footstool combination provided extra legroom and created the opportunity for passengers to customize their own space on the aircraft. Movable privacy screens meant travellers could work, rest and play free from intrusion.

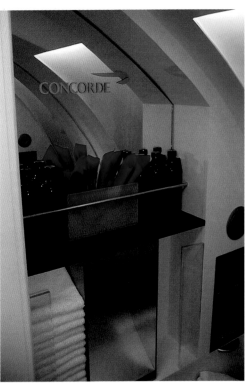

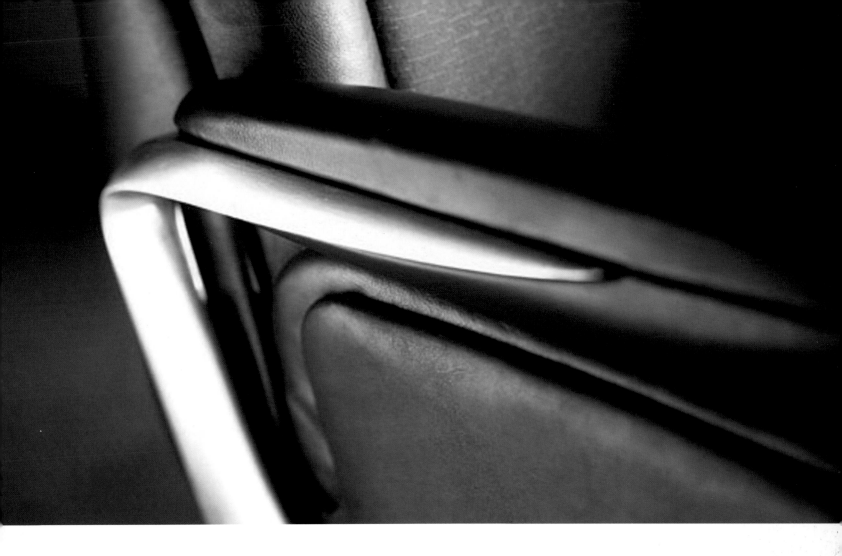

Future concepts in air travel concentrate on passenger capacity. The French aeronautical developer Aérospatiale Matra is working on a 'flying wing' that will carry 1,000 passengers. On an amphibian theme, Russian seaplane builders Beriev are constructing a series of enormous flying-boats that they hope will compete with Airbus and Boeing – using seaports as opposed to crowded airports. Lockheed Martin is developing the Aerocraft; more than three times the length of the A3XX and as wide as the A3XX is long. The Aerocraft will be part-plane, part-helium balloon and with a proposed capacity of 4,000 passengers, the queues at passport control almost defy imagination. What this entails for interior design of aircraft we can only guess at.

The early battle of the 1920s and 30s to attract customers to the skies is still competitive and thriving today, yet with all the changes in cabin interiors down the years one fact remains: legroom at the back of the aircraft doesn't increase. More space, more softness and more function is made available for the high fare-paying business and first-class set, whose passenger count is increasing and making more profit for the airlines. So, as the world gets smaller and richer, the social culture in the skies is reflecting the terrestrial trend – the only way it seems to get comfortable in flight is to pay for it.

The interior of the British Airways Concorde has been redesigned for the new millennium.

ABOVE A lighter weight seat incorporates the 'speedmarque' motif to reflect the corporate identity.

FACING BOTTOM The 1980s Concorde interior.

FACING TOP Product design consultancy Factory inspected the gutted fuselage; and the designers full-scale mock-ups of the proposed design for the new 'bathroom'.

identity

My first experience of being aware of an airline corporate identity was enhanced by the fact that it was nearly Christmas. It was late-December 1966, and I was delighted to see that the Boeing my brother and I were due to board sported a festive Christmas tree painted on the tailfin. In fact, the airline that my father had procured free tickets for that day was MEA. Middle East Airlines was, and still is, the national airline of the Lebanon and the 'Christmas tree' was a cedar of Lebanon motif in green on a white background. To further delight the demob-happy schoolboy, there was a distinct aroma of pine needles as we stepped aboard the Boeing – or it may have been the steward's pungent aftershave.

Most airlines have a logo, a convention which began in 1919 when a predecessor of Lufthansa, Deutsche Luft Reederei, applied a flying crane motif that in only a slightly modified form is still the anchor of a very successful identity history for Lufthansa. To achieve premium-brand status, and thereby win loyal custom from business and occasional travellers alike is the goal for any airline, and graphic design alone is not the solution. The logo and aircraft livery represents a small part of the identity process. There is equal importance attached to communicating the brand identity via aircraft interiors, airport lounges and gates, corporate literature, tickets, uniforms and ground vehicles. In addition to the aesthetic aspect, it is increasingly important to consider management ethos and customer service as part of the image review.

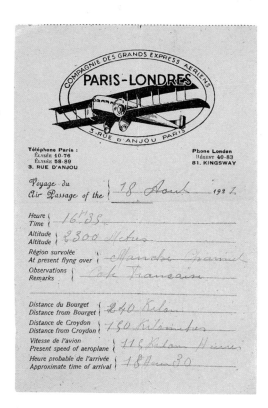

The early identities of the 1920s were 'designed' by signwriters and were rendered simply in an easy-to-read typeface. The aircraft registration codes on the wings, fuselage and tailfins were far more apparent. Air Union, however, the precursor to Air France, emblazoned its name in huge capital letters on the underbelly of its Loiré and Olivier aircraft. In clear weather, and in the days when aircraft buzzed overhead at a relatively low altitude of 1,500 feet, advertising on the aircraft itself succeeded for the duration of the flight. Royal emblems played a part in early identities. KLM (Koninklijke Luchtvaart Maatschappij) – Royal Dutch Airlines – used its royal warrant, an emblem it still retains in the guise of a simplistic crown. Flags represented national pride and in the case of Imperial Airways, the Air Ensign incorporating the Union Jack was raised through a hatch in the roof of the Short Bros. Scylla and MP42 biplanes in 1936. In the same year, on the tailfin of Lufthansa's Junkers Ju 52, the Nazi swastika in black on a white circle and red background 'advertised' the national popularity of the Third Reich, while Swissair's DC-2s sported a white cross on a red background that still adorns their aircraft today.

Across the Atlantic, American Airlines and Continental Airlines used the national symbol of the eagle, while some domestic airlines, such as National Air Transport Inc., continued the heritage of aviation as a postal service with the application of an arrow. Among other popular 'speed' symbols was Mercury, the Roman messenger of the gods, with his winged-heels for Interstate Airlines. Other American domestic carriers opted for regional symbols – the mounted cowboy

FACING Aki Alma, a show girl at the Stardust Hotel-Casino, Las Vegas, stands on the wing of a Boeing 737 with her 37-foot likeness in the background. The plane was part of the Western Pacific Airlines 'Airlogo' programme, in which the carrier used the exteriors of its aircraft for advertising.

ABOVE The steady hand of a signwriter puts the finishing touches to the British European Airways logo, 1950s.

Collectable luggage-label art
from the 1920s to the 1950s.

WESTERN AIR LINES
AMERICA'S OLDEST AIRLINE

UNITED AIR LINES

SCANDINAVIAN AIRLINES SYSTEM

MOHAWK AIRLINES
The Route of the Air Chiefs

Fly TWA Constellation
TRANS WORLD AIRLINES
Litho in U.S.A.

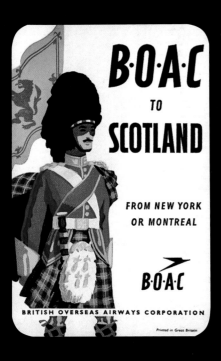

B·O·A·C TO SCOTLAND
FROM NEW YORK OR MONTREAL
B·O·A·C
BRITISH OVERSEAS AIRWAYS CORPORATION
Printed in Great Britain

TWA
THE LINDBERGH LINE

IMPERIAL AIRWAYS

WING YOUR WAY WITH
AUSTRALIAN NATIONAL AIRWAYS

ABOVE The national emblem of Switzerland adorns the tailfins of Swissair's DC-2s at Croydon Airport, UK, c.1935 and on a travel agent's promotional poster in the mid-1950s.

FACING Belgium's national carrier promotes a caring message and announces that, 'You are in good hands with Sabena,' 1950.

for Wyoming Air Service and Inland Air Lines, and the Red Indian Chief for Western Air Express. Pan American World Airways, which began life in 1927, pioneered routes across the world's oceans and continents and eventually earned the marque of a linear globe with PAN AM in extended capitals in its centre – as if to announce global domination, at least in commercial aviation terms.

Today's airlines still turn to symbolism to distinguish themselves. The Aer Lingus shamrock reflects the ideal of Ireland as a green and rural land, with the added value of a good luck charm. Greece's Olympic Airways use the olympic rings, one of the oldest cultural identities and a paragon of healthy competition. Some budget airlines get right to the point by conveying the cheapest way to get from A to B. In the 1970s, Freddie Laker's no-nonsense Skytrain had a suggestion of nationalism by incorporating elements of the British flag. Two decades later, the expertise of corporate identity consultants Wolff Olins shone through with their fresh and direct branding of BA's cheap yet chic operator, Go.

A pair of wings or a bird have always been a graphic designer's favourite influence, whether used in a military-air-force-style as on pilots' caps and badge insignia, or in a more realistic way like the flying goose for Canadian Airways (which dates from 1928). More stylized wings were devised – Air France with a graceful winged seahorse; a winged kangaroo for Australia's

ABOVE LEFT Magazine advertising for United Aircraft Corporation, early 1950s and Boeing Jetliners, early 1960s.

LEFT Posters for the Lufthansa travel agent and ticket office, 1950s.

RIGHT Pan American, 1957; Air Union, early 1920s; Air France, c.1953; Imperial Airways, 1932; BOAC (India), c.1952; BOAC (Britain), 1965.

Ever since I became the first lady jockey, I ride Braniff.
(When you got it—flaunt it.)

I said I'd make it and
And I like other people who keep trying
That's why I switched to B
I like the way their planes are painted, and I love the inte
because they don't look like every othe a
I think the Braniff girls act like they love the
And they served me really too much
(But I'll still make my we
There were lots of ice cubes available for d
and the coffee tasted like coffee should
And we got to our destination on
(For all of 1968, Braniff had a better on-time re
than any other airline in the l
Until somebody else goes them one b
I'll always ask my Travel A
"Does Braniff fly there too? Put me c
Diane Crump

national airline, Qantas; and the speedbird logo for Imperial Airways. Theyre Lee-Elliot, the designer of the original speedbird logo, may have been surprised at the polemics that his design has created in both airline enthusiast circles and in high-level design consultancy meetings. The famous logo, so indicative of Imperial Airways and subsequently BOAC, first appeared on a de Havilland Albatross in 1937. It was, however, dropped by the American design consultants Landor Associates when they were redesigning British Airways' corporate identity in 1984, in favour of a pseudo-heraldic coat of arms on a dark-blue background incorporated into a red striped design that the consultancy dubbed the 'speedwing'. The controversy that followed led June Fraser, the President of the Society of Industrial Artists and Designers, to write a letter to *The Times* newspaper, saying: 'It is alarming that the corporate identity proposed for our national airline, relying as it does upon a barely distinguishable heraldic device perched incongruously above the remnants of the earlier instantly recognizable and appropriate solution, should shortly, and at great expense to the taxpayer, be the image of this country on the tarmacs of the world.' National airlines change their identities at their own peril.

Appellations also change from decade to decade. Imperial Airways became BOAC (British Overseas Airways Corporation) and later became British Airways when it merged with BEA (British European Airways). In 1974, graphic design consultancy Negus and Negus suggested that the words 'British Airways', with 14 letters, was too long. The airline was persuaded to drop the

LEFT Magazine advertisement for Braniff International, 1969. (See pp 124 & 138.)

RIGHT Art and design of 1960: Aer Lingus, silkscreen print by Negus/Sharland. Varig, silkscreen print by Nelson Jungbluth. Qantas, litho print by Harry Rogers. El Al, litho print by Kor.

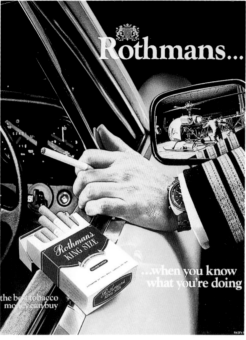

In the days before government health warnings, smoking at 35,000 feet was fashionable.

ABOVE Peter Stuyvesant's byline, 'The International Passport to Smoking Pleasure' was very successful and had thousands of smokers buying the 200 duty-free allowance, 1960s.

ABOVE CENTRE Precision engineering and total control are the lures for Rothman's King Size.

ABOVE RIGHT Filter tips all round at cocktail hour on a flight from JFK International, New York, 1951.

RIGHT Give-away ashtrays complemented the British European Airways' branded Super Virginias, mid-1950s.

Airline mementos: chrome Douglas DC-2 and glass ashtray, Swissair, late 1930s; chrome and ceramic lighter from BOAC, 1950s; delicate paper and bamboo fan from BOAC, late 1950s.

全日空

ABOVE The Japanese flag and Japanese calligraphy brand an All Nippon Airways Boeing 747.

FACING The Playboy logo adorned the tailfin of Hugh Hefner's private all-black 'Big Bunny' Douglas DC-9.

word 'Airways' and for a decade 'the World's favourite airline' (as its slogan went) was known simply as 'British'.

A further derivation of the terms 'speedbird' and 'speedwing' was 'speedmarque', devised by identity and design consultants Newell and Sorrell, and launched by British Airways in 1997. Yet more consternation was aired by nationalists and traditionalists as Newell and Sorrell not only further developed the sharp, straight-edged essence of Lee-Elliot's early 'speedbird' into a fluid ribbon, but also used the tailfin as an artist's canvas rather than a space to depict the national flag and the company's logo. The concept behind the collection of 'World Images' on the tailfins of the British Airways fleet was one of world citizenship, as explained by Newell and Sorrell's press release: 'Through a unique programme of global research, Newell and Sorrell have collated the first phase of the British Airways Collection of World Images by inviting painters, sculptors, ceramicists, weavers, quilters, calligraphers and paper artists to produce a series of "uplifting celebrations" of their own community.' The new identity followed three years of extensive research by British Airways and a further two years of research and branding by the consultancy. Alas, neither the media nor the British cultural establishments were ready for such creative 'graffiti'. In the end, British Airways responded to corporate and political opinions by painting only 50 per cent of its fleet with 'World Images' and reinstating elements of the Union Jack on the remaining aircraft.

Newell and Sorrell was not the first design agency to use the aircraft as an artist's canvas. Dallas-based Braniff International Airways made its mark due to the creative flair of Mary Wells. In 1964, with the help of her creative partners Dick Rich and Stewart Greene, Wells adopted the idea of a fully conceptual approach to advertising and marketing with a famous 'flying colors' campaign. They applied that ideal to Braniff and in 1965, employed Alexander Girard to create a new visual look for the airline – the corporate identity became synonymous with the Braniff name. Both bold verbal statements and bold visual statements reinvented Braniff as a truly modern and forward-looking commercial airline. Girard's influences were of the New World – the Aztecs, Incas, Mayas and Hopis – and from Latin America. In contrast to traditional fuselage decoration – which normally took its cue from the shape of the aircraft itself by using elongated stripes down the side, for example – Girard selected seven colours and painted whole fuselages in them and placed his Hopi-style bird logo on a white tailfin to contrast with the mass of colour. Girard also designed 56 different seat fabrics, and the new corporate identity was taken through to ticket counters, departure lounges and the new Braniff International Clubrooms. The bold 'flying colors' campaign was later echoed in Braniff's 1973 move to appoint Alexander Calder, the originator of mobile and kinetic art, to use a DC-8 aircraft as his canvas. Calder painted several scale models before Braniff engineers and draftsmen transferred the design to the full-sized jets. Sadly, as in the case of Pan Am in 1991, Braniff International finally succumbed to global competition and operations ceased in 1982.

More 'aircraft-as-canvas' concepts followed later in the mid-1990s, when Australian design studio Balarinji created the 'Nalanji Dreaming' and 'Wunala Dreaming' designs for Qantas. Both were painted in Aboriginal-inspired contemporary styles and brightened up many a drab runway. The original kangaroo symbol that appeared on Qantas aircraft was adapted from the Australian one penny coin. The design also featured as the centrepiece of the roundel adopted by the Royal Australian Air Force in 1956, and has since been adopted by all Australia's armed forces. The kangaroo was painted just below the cockpit of Qantas' first Liberator aircraft during its conversion at Brisbane's Archerfield airport in 1944, following Qantas' decision to name its Indian Ocean passage, the Kangaroo Service. The winged kangaroo symbol was created by Sydney-based designer Gert Sellheim, and first appeared in January 1947 to coincide with the introduction of Lockheed Constellations. In 1984, the flying kangaroo lost its wings once again when the Lynn Design Group refined the logo into a slender, stylized presentation. And in 1975, yet another derivation of the marsupial was designed by Ken Cato to mark Qantas' 75th anniversary year.

Historically, few logos have survived the critical eyes of the marketing and design departments. Lufthansa, however, despite the Third Reich's intervention and subsequent bankruptcy after the war has retained its flying crane logo since 1926. In the past, Lufthansa's identity has been construed as being somewhat severe, with its grey colours and 'cold' Helvetica typeface. It does,

however, exude a feeling of efficiency and safety. In response to market perception, Lufthansa decided to freshen its image. Yellow and blue was used to present a more sympathetic identity and a blue stripe was removed from the side of the aircraft to leave a clean, white fuselage. As a finale to the redesign, the flying-crane logo was modified slightly to make it more personable.

Airline identity has not always been confined to commercial airlines. In 1963, Raymond Loewy, the prolific industrial designer responsible for shaping so many commercially successful products, joined forces with John F. Kennedy to design a new exterior livery for Air Force One, the presidential Boeing 707. Their collaboration included creative sessions on the Oval Office floor, cutting out coloured-paper shapes and discussing various ideas. Kennedy was pleased with the results and asked Loewy to decorate his and Jackie's stateroom on board the aircraft. Loewy's other aviation commissions were more mainstream, however, and included designing the connecting globes for TWA and redevelopment work for the United Airlines logo.

Airlines have sometimes approached the business of corporate identity light-heartedly. Bobby Kooka, the man who conceived the Maharajah character that has promoted Air-India so endearingly over the years, has said of his creation: 'We call him a Maharajah for want of a better description. But his blood isn't blue. He may look like royalty, but he isn't royal.' The Maharajah, who bears an uncanny resemblance to Kooka, who in turn happened to be Air-India's Commercial

FACING Landor Associates' bold identity for Northwest Airlines of Minneapolis, USA, 1989. The simple design strategy combined contrasting colours quickly recognizable on the runway and large capitals on the fuselage.

ABOVE & RIGHT Since the early 1950s, Cathay Pacific has grown to become Hong Kong's leading carrier. Corporate identity designers Landor Associates explain that the 'brushwing' symbol, a single calligraphic stroke, expresses a balance of Asian heritage with modernity and proficiency, 1994.

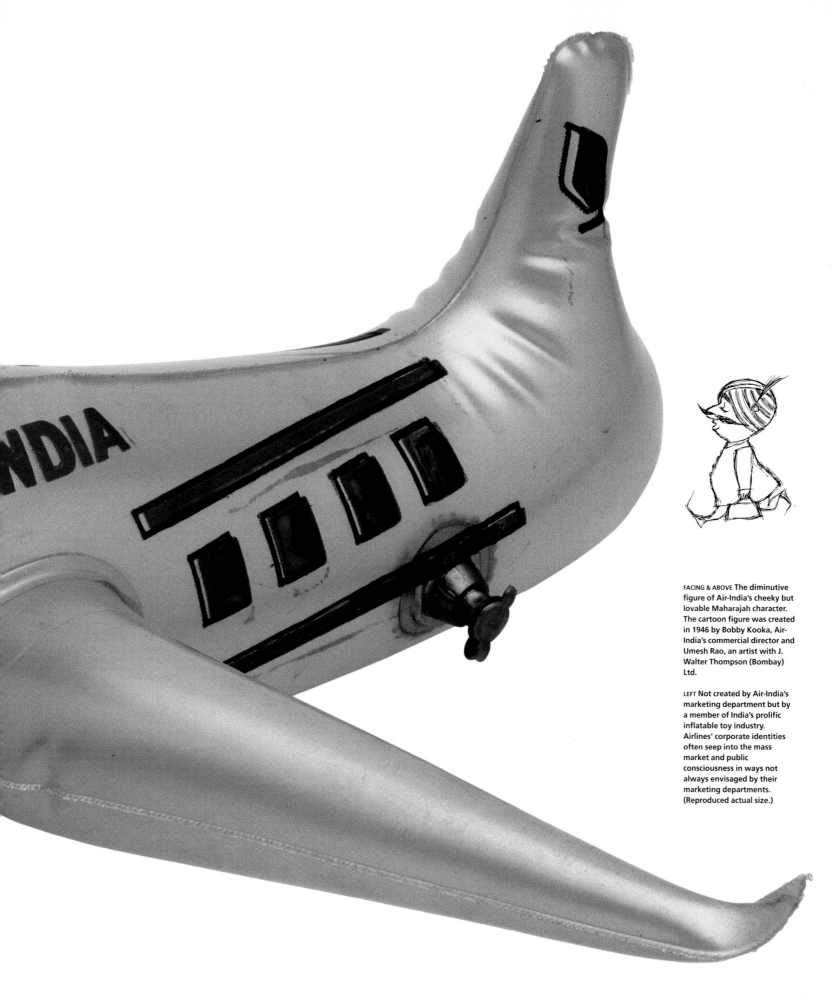

FACING & ABOVE The diminutive figure of Air-India's cheeky but lovable Maharajah character. The cartoon figure was created in 1946 by Bobby Kooka, Air-India's commercial director and Umesh Rao, an artist with J. Walter Thompson (Bombay) Ltd.

LEFT Not created by Air-India's marketing department but by a member of India's prolific inflatable toy industry. Airlines' corporate identities often seep into the mass market and public consciousness in ways not always envisaged by their marketing departments. (Reproduced actual size.)

ABOVE & FACING, TOP Independent designers, Thomas Eriksson and Björn Kusoffsky opted for the cleanliness and modernity of Rotis Sans Serif for their bold typographic approach to the livery for SAS, 1999.

LEFT & FACING, BOTTOM Founded in the 1920s, Brazil's pioneering airline, Varig, was given a completely new image by Landor Associates in 1996. The dark blue tailfin background suggested classic tradition while gold and yellow denoted the allure and warmth of the Brazilian sunshine. The 'compass rose' symbol portrayed the airline's worldwide expansion of destinations. The colours, tones and fabrics of the aircraft interiors expressed the identity's warmth and sophistication.

OVERLEAF With just a hint of nationalism and a simple but very smart livery, the majestic bulk of a British Overseas Airways Corporation Boeing 747 leaves the runway.

EURO TRAVELLER
BRITISH AIRWAYS

BRITISH
AIRWAYS

FIRST
BRITISH AIRWAYS

LEFT Class distinction: Newell and Sorrell's corporate identity for British Airways in 1997 heralded a 'New British Airways for the new Millennium,' until media and establishment opinions tempered implementation (see p122).

ABOVE & FACING Fifteen 'World Images' were collated by inviting painters, sculptors, ceramicists, weavers, calligraphers, quilters and paper artists to produce a series of 'uplifting celebrations' of their own communities. Emmly Masanabo's (Ndebele People, South Africa) painted panel, (ABOVE) and Dutch artist, Hugo Kaagman's Delft-esque motifs, (FACING) and works of other artists appeared on tailfins as well as other different points of the customer experience.

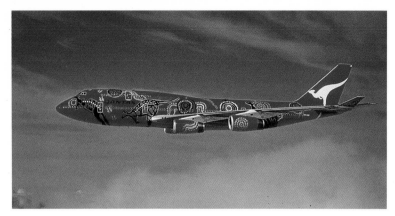

Director, was drawn by Umesh Rao, an artist with J. Walter Thompson (Bombay) Ltd, in 1946. Initially, the Kooka-Rao duo created the diminutive figure as an element on an inflight memo pad. Somewhere in the process, his creators gave him a personality: an outsized moustache, a striped turban and an aquiline nose. He became the naughty ambassador in charge of sales and promotion of Air-India's global identity. He has won numerous awards for originality in publicity due to his antics – sumo wrestler in Japan, hookah-smoker in Saudi Arabia and lover boy in Paris, for example. He is the traveller's friend and exudes warmth and hospitality – always with wit.

In the advertising and publicity of today's airline industry, there is a distinct lack of wit which probably has something to do with the serious business of market research. There is a belief that an airline's corporate identity should convey safety above all other considerations and that design should not offend anyone and appeal to everyone. At one end of the design spectrum, there is the expertly executed clarity of the 'Bauhaus' school that Lufthansa has adopted to such great success, and at the other end is the brazen creativity of Braniff, and Newell and Sorrell's British Airways. And in the middle there is the middle ground of the safe, reliable and tried-and-tested formula which appeals to the airline decision-makers and to the anonymous, average customer. Unfortunately, due to timidity and market research, the lowest common denominator wins every time, and in the judicious words of corporate-identity guru, Wally Olins, 'A company gets the corporate identity it deserves.'

FACING TOP (CLOCKWISE FROM TOP LEFT): Qantas Aboriginal livery (see p128); one of Southwest Airlines' 'State Flag' fleet; Alexander Calder's design for Braniff International Airways (see p124) and Snoopy and friends promoting the skiing season on an All Nippon Airways Boeing 747.

FACING BOTTOM Aquatic theme-park livery takes on the character and markings of Shamu the killer whale and creates advertising revenue for Southwest Airlines.

TOP Lipsmackin', thirstquenchin' Concorde refuels at Dubai in 1996. Pepsi's Concorde was leased from Air France for a whirlwind marketing tour of the Middle East as part of a $500 million project to win back market shares from arch-rival Coca-Cola.

ABOVE In 1963, a collaboration between John F. Kennedy and industrial designer Raymond Loewy led to the livery redesign of the presidential Boeing 707, Air Force One. The design was retained for a later Boeing 747 replacement, shown here (see p130).

acknowledgements

With thanks to Laurence King, Jo Lightfoot, Felicity Awdry and Laura Willis at Laurence King Publishing and a special thanks to Paul Harron for his editorial creativity and encouragement.

A sincere thanks to Alistair White for his historical guidance and allowing me access to his prized collection of ephemera.

This book is dedicated to Gilly.

I would like to thank the following people for their time and assistance:

Stephanie Arrons (British Airways), Paul Babb, Adrian Berry (Factory), Jitender Bhargava (Air-India), Nicole Böttcher (LTU), John Brindley (IATA), Neil Cavagan (Newell and Sorrell), Andrea Clinard (Southwest Airlines), Hannelie Coetzee (South African Airways), Maureen Cowdroy (for additional picture research), Isobel Czarska, Wendy Dagworthy (Royal College of Art), Martin Darbyshire (Tangerine), Brendan Dawes, Britt Dione (Landor Associates), Kim Earnest, Youssef Eddini (KLM), Sarah Edwards (Air New Zealand), Marc Essingler (Frog), Patrick Farrell (Raymond Loewy International), Dennis Fernandez (British Airways), Richard Ford (Landor Associates), Louise French (Wolff Olins); Ghislaine Giroux (ICAO), Gudren Gorner (Lufthansa), Terry Grover (Singapore Airlines), Alex Hall (Mattel UK), Gill Hasson, Erik Heath, Hugh Hefner (Playboy Enterprises), Holger Hegendorfer (IATA), Claire Henderson (Landor Associates), Paul Hiscock, Caroline Homeyard (Virgin Airways), Peter Hope Lumley, Sunathee Isvarphornchai (Thai Airways), Kaoru Jikihara (All Nippon Airways), Douglas Johnson (Gulf Air), Fred Kelley (Boeing), Stuart Lee (British Airways), Simon Lince (for his mathematics), Conway Lloyd Morgan (for his paragraph and for introducing me to Starck), Edward Lovegrove (for additional research), Gilly Lovegrove (for her relentless encouragement), Nancy Lovegrove (for her picture research in Tokyo), Thomas Lubbesmeyer (Boeing), Miss Ludewig (Lufthansa), Debbie Maclean (CAA), Graham Marsh, Nora McNeil (Southwest Airlines), Bianca Meyer (Frog), Ada Morales (Landor Associates), Sam Nakomura, Daryl Newman (All Nippon Airways), Marc Newson, Ian Nicholson, Philip Olden, Kate Opekar (All Nippon Airways), Natalia Price-Cabrera, Marshall Pumphrey, Lucy Quigley (Tangerine), Prasada Rao (Air-India), James Reid (*Wallpaper*), Annegret Richter and Mr Rudolph (Lufthansa), Markus Roozendal, Christel Roques (Airbus Industrie), Catherine Rosec (Air France), Tom Samson (Croydon Airport Society), Raj Saund (British Airways), Jeanne Schryver (Playboy Enterprises), Martin Sillwood (Japan Airlines), Sue Smallwood (for her initial encouragement), Stuart Spicer, Babbet Stapel, Sarah Stevens (Wolff Olins), Iain Stewart (Alpha Catering), Dave Sutton, H.Toba (Japan Airlines), Pikulkaew Thanompichai (Thai Airways), Alexandra Thompson (British Airways), Kathie Turin, Lorna Wain (BAA), Lucy Ward, Laurie Warner (Southwest Airlines), Rachel West (American Airlines), Adam White (Factory), Jonathan White, Fiona Wilson and Ian Wood (Landor Associates), Paul Wylde (British Airways), Bob Young (Ideal Image), Carlos Yudica, Andrea Zannoni (Alitalia).

The author and publishers would like to thank all the companies, individuals and photographers whose work is reproduced. The following photographic credits are given, with page numbers in parentheses:

Advertising Archives (79 left, 90 bottom, 116 top, 120 top left); Aer Lingus (119); Airbus Industrie (104); Alistair White Collection, photographed by Bob Young (13 bottom, 62 top, 65 top, 73 bottom, 84 top left and bottom, 85, 88 top left, 89 top, 90 bottom, 98 top right, 99 bottom, 108, 109 bottom, 114 right, 115, 117, 120 bottom, 121); Alitalia (43 top right); All Nippon Airways (2/3, 26 left, 75 top, 76/77, 122, 138); American Airlines (9, 71, 93 bottom); Andrew Toms Collection, photographed by Bob Young (73 top); British Airways Archive issued by Adrian Meredith (14/15, 18, 19 top left, 25, 34 bottom, 35, 37, 41 bottom, 50, 58, 59, 62 bottom, 63, 64/65, 68, 69 top, 74 bottom, 75 bottom, 78/79, 80, 84 top right, 86, 88, 90 top, 91, 94, 111); Boeing (82/83, 102); Corbis/Bettman UPI (front cover, 6, 10/11, 33, 36, 134/135); Croydon Airport Society (114 left); Edward Lovegrove (144); El Al (119); Factory (106, 107); Gulf Air (46/47, 79 right); Henry Hessner (91 bottom); Hulton Getty (8, 12, 19 bottom, 24, 30 top, 31 top, 32, 38, 39 top right, 48, 54/55, 60 bottom, 120 top right); Icelandair (34 top right); Japan Airlines (26/27, 28/29, 69 bottom); KLM (60 top, 61, 109 top); Landor Associates (126, 127, 128, 129, 132, 133, back cover); LTU (39 bottom); Lufthansa (13 top, 20/21, 30 bottom, 34 top left, 57, 66, 67, 70, 72 bottom, 92, 93 top, 95, 98 bottom, 99 top, 116 bottom, 99, 116 bottom, 124, 125); Marc Newson (103); Mattel UK Ltd (50/51); Newell and Sorrell (136, 137); Playboy Enterprises (100, 101, 123); Popperfoto (16/17, 19 top right, 22/23, 40, 41 top, 43 top left, 51, 56, 81, 83 top right and bottom, 89 bottom, 110, 139 top); Qantas (93 bottom, 119, 138); Raymond Loewy International (139); Rex (39 top left, 49 top); SAS (42, 133); Singapore Airlines (49 bottom, 93 bottom, 98 top left); Southwest Airlines (138); Stuart Spicer (110); Tangerine (105); Thai Airways (44/45, 74 top); Varig (119); Virgin (43 bottom, 72 top, 96, 97).

bibliography   www

Books:

Allen, Oliver E., *The Airline Builders* (Time-Life, 1981)

Allen, Roy, *SIA Take-off to Success* (Singapore Airlines, 1990)

Bean, Barbara, *Of Magic Sails* (United Airlines/Graphic Alliance, 1975)

Brindley, John F., *Wings for the World* (IATA, 1995)

Coster, Graham, *Corsairville: The Last Domain of the Flying Boat* (Viking, 2000)

Harper, Harry, *The Romance of a Modern Airway* (Sampson Low, 1930)

Hessner, Henry, *Comet Highway* (John Murray, 1953)

James, Capt. JWG, and Stroud, John (Editorial advisers), *The World's Airways* (Odhams Press, 1951)

Johnson, Lynn and O'Leary, Michael, *En Route* (Chronicle Books, 1993)

Loewy, Raymond, *Industrial Design* (Faber and Faber, 1979)

Middleton, Don, *Civil Aviation – A Design History* (Ian Allen, 1986)

Olins, Wally, *The New Guide to Identity* (The Design Council, 1995)

Penrose, Harald, *Wings Across the World* (Cassell, 1980)

Shaw, Robbie, *Baby Boeings* (Osprey Publishing Ltd, 1998)

Spicer, Stuart, *Dream Schemes* (Airlife, 1997)

Wachtel, Joachim, *The Lufthansa Story* (Lufthansa, 1984)

Winging Our Way (Alitalia,1997)

Magazines:

Stephen Brook, 'Glass Ceiling' *Condé Nast Traveller* (February 2000)

Karen Chung, 'Balloonacy' *Wallpaper** (May/June 1999)

Tim Clark, 'The Next Big Thing' *Condé Nast Traveller* (August 1999)

Laura Jacobs, 'Stewardess' *Twice* (No.2 Vol.2, 1998)

Christophe Jakubyszyn, 'Wings of Desire' *Wallpaper** (September 1999)

Julian Moxon 'Air Transport' *Flight International* (November 1999)

Cliff Nichols, 'Better by Design' *Aircraft Interiors International* (Summer 1998)

Alice Rawsthorn, 'Air Apparent' *Wallpaper** (March 1999)

Alice Rawsthorn, 'Marc1' *Wallpaper** (April 1999)

Tom Samson, 'Croydon Changes' *Aeroplane Monthly* (April 1995)

Lyndy Stout, 'Flights of Fancy' *Creative Review* (June 1997)

Henry Sutton, 'Smile High Club' *Condé Nast Traveller* (November 1998)

Stephen Wood, 'That Was Then' *Condé Nast Traveller* (February 1999)

aeroflot.com
airbus.com
airfrance.fr
air-india.com
airlines.com
airnz.com
alaskaairlines.com
americanairlines.com
ana.co.jp
ansett.com
austrianair.com
baa.co.uk
boeing.com
braniffinternational.com
braniffinternational.org
britishairways.com
cathaypacific.com
cdnair.com
china-airlines.com
csa.cz
delta-air.com
ebay.com
factorydesign.co.uk
flycontinental.com
frogdesign.com
gulfairco.com
iata.org
icao.int
iflyswa.com
interbrand.com
jal.co.jp
lanchile.cl
landor.com
lufthansa.com
manx-airlines.com
mea.com.lb
nwa.com

panam.org
qantas.com
raymondloewy.com
rja.com.jo
singaporeair.com
swissair.com
tangerine.net
twa.com
ual.com
usairways.com
virgin-atlantic.com
wolff-olins.com
worldair.com

index

OVERLEAF **The author's parents, Edward and Babs Lovegrove, and brother Steven, about to board a BOAC Bristol Britannia flight from Khartoum, Sudan, to London in 1956.**